Navigation Book.

Learn How To Find Your Way Without Map
Or Modern Technologies

Table of Content

Introduction 3

Chapter 1 – Asking for directions 5

Chapter 2 – Know how to navigate roads 7

Chapter 3 – The moss 9

Chapter 4 – Good ol' needle and magnet trick 11

Chapter 5 – Follow the rivers 14

Chapter 6 – Use the stars 16

Chapter 7 - Use the sun 18

Chapter 8 – Use a watch 20

Chapter 9 – Clues from nature & civilization 21

Chapter 10 – Landmarks 23

Conclusion 25

Introduction

Human beings are a migratory species at heart. Generally we have only recently- in evolutionary terms- begun staying in one place for extended periods of time. This... isn't really normal for us, and we generally do try to travel every now and then. It's in our instincts to do so. You most definitely at some time will find yourself traveling away from home.

If you are traveling, it's possible that you could end up lost. And if you are lost, you'll need to find your way home or to your destination. Modern convenience has afforded us the GPS and the map and the compass to do this-- and most of us don't even use the map or compass anymore, which is a terrible shame. Navigation is something we usually take for granted... up until the point where we actually need to get somewhere on our own. Then it seriously becomes an issue.

Luckily, our ancestors have been finding their way around the planet for hundreds of thousands of years just with a general sense of direction, and a little help from nature. Nature itself provides ample clues about where you are in relation to everything else. The sun, the moon, the stars and the rivers all give you hints of direction and where you are going.

However you don't need to be some kind of mystic shaman to interpret the meaning of the phase of the moon and the positions of all the stars-- if you're a modern person, you probably already know what continent you are on, and what hemisphere you are in. You have a serious leg up over our ancient ancestors, even without a GPS. So finding your way should be a breeze, really.

Granted, you're not going to be able to find your exact longitude and latitude by turning over a stone or letting sand fall from your hand; that's impossible stuff that they do in the movies.

But there are a few basic tips and tricks that you can use to better get a direction of where you are going when you need to. Whether you ever have to use skills like this or not is really determined on how often you travel or might run into such trouble.

Chapter 1 – Asking for directions

Simply put, asking for directions is the most primitive way of finding your way once you're lost. Yes. You could be in the wilderness- but even in the wilderness and in situations where you may think yourself to be in some remote location... asking for directions from the odd passer-by is a skill you need to be able to have. Or rather... a pride you need to swallow.

Let's be real here. The most likely scenario where you'll be lost and need to find your way home or to your destination is when you're on a road trip and your phone dies. But you don't have a map because who does, right?

Stop at a gas station and ask them where you are and tell them where you're going. Gas station attendees are pretty knowledgeable about where the are and where major destinations are in relation to where they are. They get questions like this asked all the time, and you'll probably never see them again if you're traveling-- so you don't need to worry about embarrassing yourself in these situations.

If you're looking for a specific address, the best life-hack that you can do is ask a pizza place that does delivery. Delivery drivers and those kinds of restaurants know all the local roads and destinations, so asking them will get you the best directions to where you need to go.

Even if you're alone in the wilderness and you need to find your way back to civilization, your first priority should be trying to find someone else. Make yourself as conspicuous as possible and if it's night-time, look for light sources. Sources of light at night are almost certainly people, and the vast majority of people are good and will help you in a serious situation where you're lost.

This also means that you have to be able to speak the native dialect of wherever you are-- at least learning how to ask for directions and receive them. In the VERY least, know how to ask for someone who speaks your language, or ask for a hospital or emergency call. That's important to know no matter where you are traveling.

People connect to one another and are thus a very good resource for getting where you are going. There's no shame in stopping and asking for directions if you are lost. And that doesn't take anything other than finding someone and knowing how to speak their language. Be sure you can talk to them though!

Know where your destination is relative to other landmarks and locations of interest so that if you describe where you are going to someone they will be able to at least give you directions to the landmark.

Chapter 2 – Know how to navigate roads

This seems silly, but roads are actually something that you need to be able to interpret and navigate. There are different road sign symbols used for each region of the world, but in America all of the interstate roads with odd numbers run north and south, and all of the interstate roads with even numbers run east and west.

There's also different tricks for finding out what general direction you are going while on a road. Mile-markers are important to note, as well as the differences between a state highway and an interstate highway. State highways are less likely to follow the more strict east-west rule since they are usually roads that have been built up to highways over time out of necessity.

Road signs will usually periodically tell you what road you are on, and if you are on a small road that comes up to an intersection, you can always check what road you are on by stopping near an intersection and examining the road signs there.

You know the old saying that 'all road lead to Rome'?-- well that's not exactly wrong-- figuratively speaking that is. Most roads will lead to other larger roads, and most every large road will lead to a city of some type.

If you find a road while you are lost in the wilderness, then following that road will invariably lead to some type of civilization. There are also very, very few roads in the world that are not regularly traveled by other people-- so you will be able to flag down someone else on that road if you need to.

Just avoid dirt roads-- while dirt roads are still good roads to follow to find civilization if you are lost in the wilderness, they are sometimes temporary or rarely-traveled roads that go into the wilderness.

Logging companies will form temporary dirt roads in order to access natural timber. Sometimes these dirt roads go on for miles and miles, so if you pick the wrong direction to go down when you come across these, it could be leading you further into the wilderness than you were before.

However, even dirt roads are far preferable to trudging your way around in a forest looking for your way home or to your destination-- so if you find a dirt road, you can follow it until you find some other path or road.

It's also notable to mention that deer can form 'roads' or trampled paths of their own that may seem like dirt roads but actually aren't and don't lead anywhere with people in them. So there is a very small chance that you can stumble upon one of these-- which typically don't go on for that long-- that can stand to get you even more lost than you already were.

Chapter 3 – The moss

Moss only grows in the shade. Well... the kinds of moss that have sort of a 'slimy' texture when you feel them. Not the kinds of gray moss that hangs from trees; that grows all around the trees and feeds off of the breeze of the air.

But the kind of lichen that's slimy only grows in the constant shade; exposure to direct sunlight will kill that kind of moss very quickly, so it needs the constant cool shade in order to live and thrive. This, however, can give you a great tip on direction.

In the northern hemisphere, moss will only grow on the north side of large trees and rocks, because of the tilt of the earth. So if you're lost and you need to know which way is north, you can always look to the cool slimy moss on the sides of things if there's any around and you don't have a clear view of the sky or anything quite like that.

There are better ways of finding north-- and finding north by itself isn't particularly useful unless you have some scope or idea of where you are traveling beforehand.

If you are looking at a group of trees or a wall or a rock and there's moss on it, you will be able to notice that the moss is only on one side - that side is always north in the northern hemisphere.

In the southern hemisphere, the moss will typically only grow on the south side of trees and rocks and such.

However, this can be messed up if you're in an area that's got a sufficient amount of shade all the time. If there's a very thick forest canopy overhead then you may find that moss can grow everywhere.

Or if you are in a cave then there's not exactly any particular way to tell from the moss which direction is north. Because odds are moss will be everywhere if you are in a cave.

Chapter 4 – Good ol' needle and magnet trick

Earth has a magnetic field that runs north and south. Magnetized objects are sensitive to this field and will align themselves accordingly to this field if there's low enough friction for them to do so.

We've probably heard about this trick in the boy-scouts, but the specifics of it have seldom been laid out to us so that we can remember exactly how to do it. Essentially you can make a make-shift compass with a thin piece of metal and a permanent magnet.

You still have to have a magnet... which... you might not have-- but some purses have magnetic clasps that you can use, and even some reading glasses have magnets in them-- so there's a small chance you might have a magnet on you without even knowing. It is possible to make a magnet out of a car battery, but we're not going to get into that since it's possible that you could harm yourself while attempting that.

So don't fiddle with car batteries when you're lost unless you absolutely know what you're doing.

But if you can find a permanent magnet, and you also have a needle, or a thin piece of magnetic wire such as a paper-clip bent straight... you can magnetize the paper-clip

To magnetize your paper-clip, you simply need to continue to rub the magnet back and forth on it as if you were 'sharpening' the paper-clip if that makes sense.

Stroke the magnet from one end of the paper clip to the other and continue doing this about 40-100 times. Once you are done, the paper clip will be slightly magnetic. You can test this to see if it lightly touches or sticks to magnetic surfaces.

Now find a leaf or a thin slice of cork and a body of still water. It could be a lake or a cup of water or something of that sort. In fact, it doesn't even have to be water; any liquid will do-- even a bowl of just vinegar.

Place the magnetized needle on the cork or leaf or whatever flotation device you have, then place that whole thing in the water. The needle will orient itself facing north and south.

Now the problem is telling which direction is north and which is south. Really, it's quite easy to get confused at this point, but if you were mindful to keep stroking the magnet in one uniform direction, the 'end' of where you were stoking the magnet is the north pole of the needle.

Sometimes it can be flipped or mixed up depending on how you hold the magnet and a number of other things; but if you have a magnet that has its north and south sides labeled, you can always test to see what side of the magnet is which by introducing the south side of your magnet to your needle. The needle will flip and be attracted to the magnet.

The end of the needle that is attracted to the south side of the magnet is the north side of the needle. Pulling the magnet away at that point and letting the needle re-orient itself is very useful for telling which direction is truly north.

However it is possible that you could have a magnet that isn't labeled. If your magnet isn't labeled then you could possibly run into the problem of not knowing which side of your needle is what pole. Even then; it's good to have that narrowed down, which gives you an orient of north and south anywhere on the globe.

This even works in caves, so you can hopefully navigate around somewhat in the cave with this method of navigation-- but it's still highly unlikely that you could be trapped underground and need to get back up to the surface.

Regular people don't get trapped underground very often, and if you're going cave or tunnel exploring, it's good to have other methods of nagivation and path-finding.

Chapter 5 – Follow the rivers

Finding civilization is easy if you've found a stream or some flowing body of water. Follow that stream to its draining body of water. Sometimes this is a lake-- but it very rarely is. Most rivers channel in to other rivers and then drain into an ocean.

Aside from that, most every large lake and certainly most land along the coast in developed countries is populated to some extent.

So if you find yourself lost but you see a stream or a river. Follow that stream or river and it will almost inevitably lead to civilization of some sort,

The myth that all rivers flow south is completely false. The Mississippi river in the United States flows south, and has a huge network of estuaries and contributing rivers that all flow in a southern-oriented direction for the most part. From this, the myth has been perpetuated that rivers flow south.

This is false. There are hundreds of examples of rivers that do not flow south or towards the equator. In fact the St. Johns river in Florida, as well as the San Joaquin river in California both flow north as examples.

And beyond that, rivers take meandering curves most of the time that can cause them to flow in a particular direction overall. This direction is not necessarily south at all times.

However, what you do need to understand about rivers or any flowing body of water is that they will always go downhill. They will follow the path of least resistance downhill until they drain into another body of water.

Most bodies of water on the planet- and certainly in developed countries- are occupied and inhabited by people. So you will be able to find people if you follow flowing water; it's just a simple safe bet.

Rivers and flowing bodies of water are also useful as modes of transportation in other less developed countries-- particularly eastern ones. So sticking nearby them is a pretty safe bet that, again, you'll run into people.

Chapter 6 – Use the stars

The stars are, for our purposes, fixed and eternal. The earth moves about as it revolves around the sun, and it also spins on its axis during this revolution around the sun. This changes the perspective that we have on the stars and makes them appear to 'move' – but it is us moving, and not the stars.

There is one star in particular that we call the 'northern star' or its proper name "Polaris."

This is a simple fact of geometry that there would be a particular star that doesn't seem to move around the northern point. In fact, the more northernly a star is in the night sky, the less it will seem to 'move' because, again, what causes stars to move across the sky is the fact that the earth is spinning.

To illustrate this concept you can take a ball and put dots on it. Spin the ball on the table. You will notice that at the top of the ball, the dots don't seem to move around that much, but the dots are a blur and move very quickly around the middle of the ball when it is spinning. This is a rough approximation of what's going on here.

This isn't very far at all from what's actually happening. In outer space, stars are more or less fixed points that are always gleaming. However, we are spinning and so the stars that are at the "top" of our spinning ball don't seem to move much at all.

Polaris is just such a star. In the northern hemisphere, you can find Polaris by first finding the big dipper. The handle of the big dipper points up toward Polaris.

Also Orion's Belt (sometimes referred to as 'The three kings') line up with Polaris, which is a pretty bright star to begin with. Polaris is always in the north of the sky and has a bright white light in comparison to other stars.

Chapter 7 - Use the sun

The sun is also a somewhat fixed point in outer space, but due to the rotation of the earth it will appear to move across the sky giving us night and day.

This simple fact means that, relative to your position on earth, the Sun will rise in the east and set in the west-- only slightly off-kilter.

If you are in the northern hemisphere, the sun will appear to be slightly to the south of the middle of the sky. If you are in the south, it will appear to cycle through the days slightly north of being directly overhead during the day. And if you are on the equator, then the sun will cast no shadows during high noon.

Pay attention to the shadows of objects that are sticking straight up. If objects that are sticking straight up cast a shadow and you are in the northern hemisphere, that shadow is pointing somewhat north. At mid-day; when the sun is highest in the sky, an object pointing straight up will cast a shadow that points straight north.

The same goes for the southern hemisphere and the southern direction. You can always use shadows to determine roughly which way is north or south by using the sun-- just the same way that sun dials work.

Another way you can use shadows and the sun is to find a shadow of an object that's not moving. Place a rock or mark where that shadow is. Then, after the shadow has moved, on the same point of the shadow (such as the tip of a stick's shadow), mark the new spot.

Then draw a line between the two spots. The line will be going east and west. The first mark is the western spot, and the second mark is the eastern spot.

The moon is somewhat less reliable but more or less follows similar rules. You cannot reliably use shadows with the moon, either. Which is a problem.

Chapter 8 – Use a watch

We've all seen this in the movies before... And here it is. Finally; you'll be able to tell which direction you're facing by using a watch with dials on it.

Don't worry if you don't have a watch with dials on it. You can always just draw out the time on like a piece of paper or something to that effect. Or if you're good enough, you can imagine a clock with dials and hands and all that floating invisibly in front of you while you do this.

In the nothern hemisphere, between the hours of 7am and 7pm... if you turn the clock so that the hour hand is pointing directly towards the sun, then half way between the hour hand and the 12 o' clock position is South.

The same thing works in the southern hemisphere but in reverse.

The reason why this works is because science.

That was a joke. But essentially what this is a short-cut to is how our ancient ancestors would be able to get their bearings by just developing a sense of where the sun should be at what time of day.

Chances are you innately have a bit of this sense already and may not even be aware that you do. However, it does change depending on where you are in the world if you've traveled far distances and find yourself lost then.

The point of this is that you'll always know your bearings so long as you can tell what time it is. But what if you can't tell what time it is...?

Chapter 9 – Clues from nature & civilization

Nature itself provides ample clues as to which direction you're facing.

Generally, in the northern hemisphere, snow will melt on the south side of hills and rocks before it will melt on the north side. If you can look at a hill that's half-covered in snow, you'll be able to tell mostly which direction is which just by looking at it.

As mentioned before, certain types of mosses and lichens will prefer to grow on the northern side of trees if there aren't peculiar conditions to cause it to grow elsewhere.

Ants will generally prefer to build their hills on the side of trees facing the equator and on the sides of hills that face the equator too.

The way clouds move in the sky tends to stay relatively consistent. You can always note which direction you are traveling relative to which direction the clouds are moving to determine whether or not you are going in circles... Of course this only works for a few hours, since wind directions can change-- but they do change much less so for clouds than they do down on the ground.

If you are lost at sea you can always follow birds if you find them since they will lead you to land-- and birds tend to fly in straight directions, so they will always give you a clue as to where to go.

However... it could be that you're not in a natural spot, and you're in fact lost in a city that you don't know.

Of course, in a city or a town, it's always best to ask for directions-- but what if it's night time or for one reason or another there just aren't people around?

Well... TV satellites will generally all point the same direction in a town. It doesn't necessarily matter which direction this is in, since just knowing that they're all pointing about the same direction is good enough to give you some perspective on whether you're going in circles or not. But in the UK, most of the TV satellites point southeast.

Religious buildings are oriented in the four cardinal directions as well. Many other types of buildings, such as Masonic Lodges also have specific orientations to them-- however we will not talk about the specifics of masonic lodges.

Roads will build up to support traffic. Most traffic in towns heads in and out of towns, so if you notice that the roads are tending to be able to carry traffic north and south, then you are probably at either the north or southern end of town.

Likewise, this works for the east and western directions. This is more for the larger traffic supporting roads than for the smaller ones. There are exceptions, but these will tend to be true and will indicate what area of town you are in.

So there's always some kind of clues that are available to you to give you a sense of direction as long as you are willing to look for those clues and pay close attention to them.

Chapter 10 – Landmarks

This will require prior knowledge to your travels.

However, you can always do a little bit of research before hand and note which direction certain high-points or landmarks may be. If there is a mountain or a peak or even a valley or large building that you can take note of, you can in the very least keep yourself from going in circles by making sure to keep your eye on that land-mark as a reference point.

However, if you know where your destination is relative to landmarks, and finding those landmarks is not a problem, then you'll always be able to find your way.

This works with directions around town-- if you can find some kind of square or very large building and then know how to get to your destination from there. And it also works when traveling in nature. If there's a large tree or something that you can always spot, and you know how to get to your destination from there, then you won't be too lost as long as you keep an eye on that tree.

Landmarks are fantastic ways of keeping your directions as concise as possible-- at sea people used to construct lighthouses to act specifically as landmarks. Light houses are still used as distinct landmarks to this day, in fact.

In fact all directions are relative-- so you'll need something as a reference point to find your destination; whether that reference point is a collection of satellites or a star or the sun or a mountain or some kind of road or highway-- you'll always be using a reference point in order to direct yourself anywhere.

So before you travel, make sure you have some type of grasp on what sorts of landmarks there are nearby. Landmarks are very handy in that regard, and you may be surprised how much easier it is to use them than you previously may have thought.

Conclusion

Getting lost is a terrible thing that happens to nearly all of us at least once in our lives. We're going to have to be able to find out which direction we're going and how to reach our destinations or in the very least retrace our steps and find our way back home at some point in our lives.

Natural navigation is an essential skill to have; and our ancestors have been perfecting it for many millennium or thousands and thousands of years if not millions of years before we even invented technology. Our ancestors would just have an innate sense of direction and where they were relative to where they needed to go. It was just... in them. And if that's true then a good sense of direction must be in you too.

In fact, some naturalists or professional hunters/trappers/outdoorsmen have this sense of where they are at all times as well. It's just a sense that comes with being outside and around a certain spot for long enough; you end up memorizing and just knowing where you are relative to where you need to be.

However, this book has outlined many of the techniques you can used when you are lost to always find your direction or 'lost-proof' yourself. You can use the cheesy techniques such as using magnetized needles floating on water, or using a watch as a sun dial-- but that isn't really necessary.

You've also learned some pretty neat little skills and tips about how to navigate towns and man-made structures such as highway roads and the like. You've learned that highways (at least in the US) are oriented east and west when they are an even number, and north and south when they are an odd number.

Similarly, the layouts of towns are so that most traffic going in and out of them will demand that the roads be large enough to carry that traffic, and thus by paying attention to the roads you'll be able to tell which end of town you probably are in. Roads are a huge help to finding your way anywhere; it's the main reason why they were invented in the first place!

(except for deer roads which you may have heard of for the first time here in this book)

You've also learned that there are navigation myths out there. You've learned that not all rivers flow south or towards the equator-- that's complete nonsense. However, most rivers do lead to people and civilization, so you'll hopefully be able to find your way to where you need to go that way.

Regardless of your method of navigation; there are plenty of these techniques here in this book that you can use to find your way.

So remember. Be prepared. And know the way.

FREE BonusReminder

Preppers Street Survival Guide
Aaron Wingazer
Proven Tactics For Armed Incounters
PreppersLiving.com

If you have not grabbed it yet, please go ahead and download your special bonus report *"Preppers Street Survival Guide: Proven Tactics For Armed Incounters"*

SimplyClicktheButtonBelow

[Click Here to Download the ebook]

OR **Go to This Page**

http://preppersliving.com/free

BONUS #2: More Free & Discounted Books & Products

Do you want to receive more Free/Discounted Books or Products?

We have a mailing list where we send out our new Books or Products when they go free or with a discount on Amazon. Click on the link below to sign up for Free & Discount Book & Product Promotions.

=> Sign Up for Free & Discount Book & Product Promotions <=

[SIGN UP NOW]

OR Go to this URL

http://zbit.ly/1WBb1Ek

Printed in Great Britain
by Amazon